PROJECTS

Falkirk Council

Fiona Macdonald

OXFORD
UNIVERSITY PRESS

OXFORD
UNIVERSITY PRESS

Great Clarendon Street, Oxford OX2 6DP

Oxford University Press is a department of the University of Oxford.
It furthers the University's objective of excellence in research, scholarship,
and education by publishing worldwide in

Oxford   New York

Auckland   Cape Town   Dar es Salaam   Hong Kong   Karachi
Kuala Lumpur   Madrid   Melbourne   Mexico City   Nairobi
New Delhi   Shanghai   Taipei   Toronto

With offices in

Argentina   Austria   Brazil   Chile   Czech Republic   France   Greece
Guatemala   Hungary   Italy   Japan   Poland   Portugal   Singapore
South Korea   Switzerland   Thailand   Turkey   Ukraine   Vietnam

Oxford is a registered trade mark of Oxford University Press
in the UK and in certain other countries

British Library Cataloguing in Publication Data

Data available

ISBN: 978-0-19-846131-9

7 9 10 8

Printed in China by Imago

Paper used in the production of this book is a natural,
recyclable product made from wood grown in sustainable forests.
The manufacturing process conforms to the environmental
regulations of the country of origin.

Acknowledgements

The publisher would like to thank the following for permission to reproduce photographs:
p6t Dorling Kindersley/Colin Keates, **p6**m Dorling Kindersley/Peter Anderson, **p6**b Ancient Art & Architecture;
p7t Werner Forman Archive, **p7**b Dorling Kindersley/Geoff Dann; **p8**t Werner Forman Archive; **p9** Ancient Art and
Architecture; **p10** Pol Foto/Denmark; **p11**t 2004 Werner Forman/Topfoto; **p11**b Richard T Nowitz/Corbis; **p12**t Ancient
Art & Architecture, **p12**b C Tait/ Ancient Art & Architecture; **p13** Werner Forman Archive/National Museum, Copenhagen;
p14 Werner Forman Archive/Universitetets Oldsaksamling, Oslo; **p15**t Topfoto/Charles Walker; **p15**b Corbis/Ted Spiegl;
p16t Ancient Art & Architecture, **p16**b Bibliotheque des Arts Decoratifs, Paris, France, Archives Charment/Bridgeman
Art Library; **p18** Werner Forman Archive/Thjodminjasafn, Reykjavik, Iceland (National Museum); **p19** Werner Forman
Archive/Thjodminjasafn, Reykjavik, Iceland; **p20**t Werner Forman Archive/University Museum of National Antiquity,
Uppsala, Sweden, **p20**m Ancient Art & Architecture, **p20**b Werner Forman Archive/Statens Historiska Museum,
Stockholm; **p21** Topfoto/Museum of London/HIP; **p23**t Heritage Image Partnership, **p23**b Ancient Art & Architecture.

Cover photograph: The British Museum

Illustrations by Carol Jonas and Brian Lee

Map illustration by Mark Duffin

Designed by Bigtop

Contents

Introduction

Who were the Vikings? Fearsome pirates? Brave warriors? Peaceful farmers? Bold explorers? Musicians? Athletes? Sailors? Kings?

Viking people were all these things, and more. Read on, and discover!

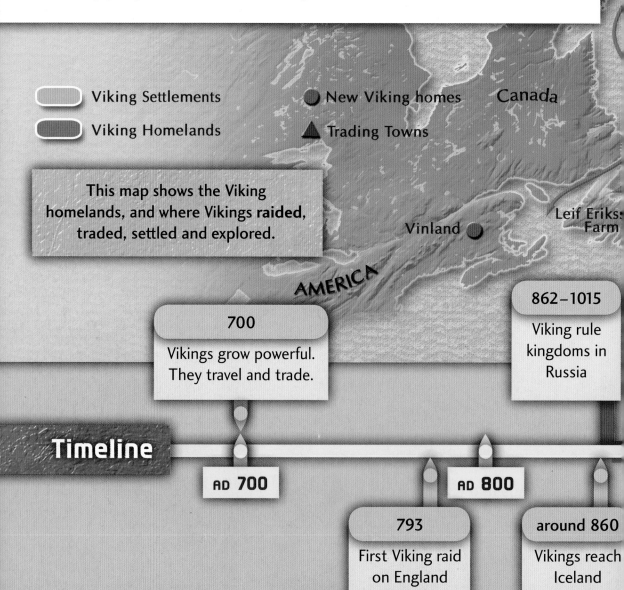

Viking Settlements

Viking Homelands

New Viking homes   Canada

Trading Towns

This map shows the Viking homelands, and where Vikings **raided**, traded, settled and explored.

Vinland

Leif Eriks: Farm

AMERICA

700

Vikings grow powerful. They travel and trade.

862–1015

Viking rule kingdoms in Russia

Timeline

AD **700**

AD **800**

793

First Viking raid on England

around 860

Vikings reach Iceland

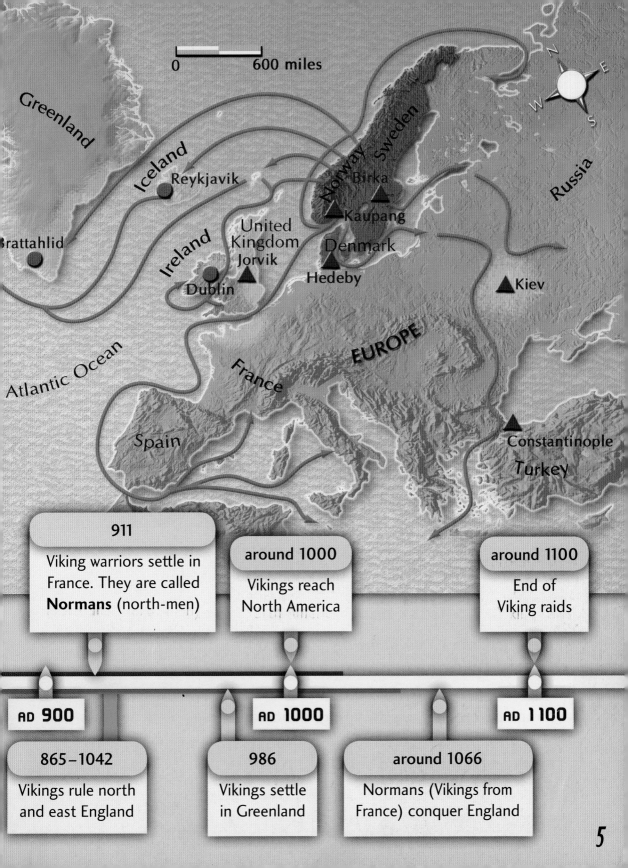

Greenland

Iceland

Reykjavik

Brattahlid

Ireland

Dublin

United Kingdom

Jorvik

Atlantic Ocean

France

Spain

Norway

Sweden

Birka

Kaupang

Denmark

Hedeby

EUROPE

Russia

Kiev

Constantinople

Turkey

0 — 600 miles

911

Viking warriors settle in France. They are called **Normans** (north-men)

around 1000

Vikings reach North America

around 1100

End of Viking raids

AD **900**

AD **1000**

AD **1100**

865–1042

Vikings rule north and east England

986

Vikings settle in Greenland

around 1066

Normans (Vikings from France) conquer England

amber

Fossil resin (gum, from pine trees that lived 30 million years before Viking times). The Vikings traded amber and used it to make jewellery.

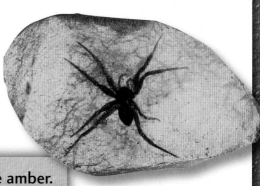

Prehistoric spider trapped inside amber.

antlers

Horns from deer. Used by Viking craft-workers to make arrow-heads, combs and needles. Vikings also used cows' horns and animal bones to make tools, weapons and jewels.

A decorated Viking comb with thin strips of antler.

berserkers (bur-sur-kurz)

Fierce warriors. The name comes from the 'bear-sarks' (bear-skin shirts) they wore. Berserkers worked themselves into a rage before battle, by singing, dancing, chanting and clashing their weapons together. Some also ate poisonous **fungi**, which made them mad for a while.

church

Building where **Christian** Vikings went to pray. The first Vikings worshipped many different gods and goddesses. After around AD 950, priests from England and Germany taught Viking people about the Christian faith and by 1200, most Vikings were Christians.

A Viking church, built of wood.

clothes

Vikings dressed well. They also needed to keep warm in winter, or when travelling at sea. Clothes were made by women using wool (from sheep), linen (from flax plants), leather (from cows and goats) and fur (from foxes, wolves, seals and bears). Rich Vikings also wore silk clothes bought from traders.

Erik the Red

Born in Iceland, but forced to run away after he killed a man. He sailed to Greenland and built the first Viking house there. In AD 986, he asked families from Iceland to join him. Together, they built two villages, which survived for almost 400 years.

Remains of Erik the Red's farmhouse on Greenland.

families

Viking families were big and busy. Children, parents and grandparents lived together in the same house, along with servants and slaves. They helped and protected each other. But when times were hard, old or weak family members might be left outside in the cold to die.

farming

Most Vikings were farmers. They grew grain, onions, peas, garlic, parsnips, cabbages, apples and herbs. They raised pigs for meat, cows and goats for milk, geese and chickens for eggs, and sheep for wool. In summer, they made hay (cut and dried grass) to feed animals during long, cold winters.

feasts

On special occasions, such as weddings or **Yule**, Vikings invited their friends to a feast. Everyone wore their best clothes, ate lots of food, told stories and jokes, danced, sang and listened to music. Viking kings held special feasts for top warriors, to celebrate their bravery.

Eating and drinking at a feast. Can you see the barbecued chicken and the drinking horn?

Ff food

Vikings ate two meals a day – in the morning and the evening. Favourite foods were meat, butter, cheese and porridge. They caught fish, whales and seals from the sea. They ate some fresh and **preserved** the rest, using salt or smoke from wood fires. Vikings hunted in mountains for deer and boar (wild pigs). They climbed cliffs to collect sea-birds' eggs, and gathered berries, nuts and mushrooms in forests. They liked to drink milk, water and beer.

Ff forts

Forts protected people from danger in wartime. The biggest forts were built by kings to defend their kingdoms from invaders.

King Harald Bluetooth built Trelleborg in Denmark around AD 980.

Frey and Freyja

Frey was the god who helped plants and animals to grow. Frey's sister, Freyja, was the goddess of love. She protected children and families.

Metal statue of Frey. Vikings said that he made the rain fall and the sun shine.

funerals

Vikings thought that the spirits of dead people travelled to the next world. So Vikings buried rich people in ships, with food, clothes, weapons, jewellery, horses and slaves beside them. Then they burned the ship or heaped earth on top of it. Vikings buried ordinary people in graves shaped like ships.

A Viking princess was buried in this reconstructed ship.

Harald Bluetooth

King of Denmark from AD 958 to 987. He was the first king to rule all of Denmark and the country's first Christian king. He built a mighty wall to keep out invaders. He died in battle.

Harald Bluetooth had this stone carved in memory of his parents.

Harald Hardrada

Tough, warlike King of Norway from AD 1046 to 1066. His name means 'hard-ruler'. He went on raids aged only 15, then fought in Russia and Constantinople (now called Istanbul, in Turkey). He died leading 300 Viking ships during an invasion of England.

A stained glass window of Harald Hardrada in Orkney, Scotland.

heroes

Vikings said, 'Glory is better than long life'. They honoured brave heroes in poems and songs. Some heroes were real, like Hastein, a pirate who sailed to Africa.

houses

Vikings built houses from wood, turf or stone. Most had one big, dark, smoky room and a heavy door. There was always a fire, for cooking and heating. People sat and slept on the floor, or on low benches covered with rugs and furs. Rich families had wooden storage chests and a 'high seat' (carved chair) for the head of the household.

A wooden Viking house with a thatched straw roof.

jewellery

Men and women liked to wear jewellery. It looked good and showed they had money. The best jewellery was made from gold or silver, but Viking craft-workers also made brooches, necklaces and rings from cheap metals, animal bones and coloured glass.

Heavy neck rings and upper-arm rings, like this one, were worn by men.

kings and chiefs

Vikings kings raided, conquered lands, fought invaders and led religious ceremonies. They were helped by chiefs, called jarls (*yarls*), Each king and chief had his own army of loyal fighting men. He rewarded them with treasure and protected their farms.

Lief Eriksson

Lief was the son of Erik the Red. Around AD 1000, he sailed from Greenland, hoping to find a land once seen by Viking sailors. Leif landed at a place he called 'Vinland' (now in Canada), and spent a winter nearby. Later, he returned with Viking settlers. They built a farm, but fought with the local people. So they left the farm and sailed home.

metalwork

Iron was the most important metal. It was used to make nails for building houses and ships, pots for cooking, farm tools, weapons and armour. Gold and silver were more valuable than iron, but less useful. They were made into jewellery and coins.

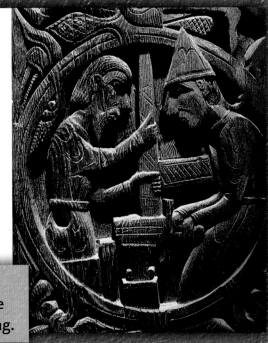

Viking blacksmiths (iron-workers) were skilful and very strong.

Odin

Terrifying god of battle. He was wise, but cruel. He could change his shape and see everything. Vikings killed horses – and humans – as offerings to please him.

Odin rode a magic eight-legged flying horse, called Sleipnir.

picture stones

Tall stones put up in memory of dead men, women and children (See Harald Bluetooth). They were carved or painted with runes and with pictures from myths and legends. Today, they tell us a lot about Viking life.

runes (roones)

Letters made from spiky straight lines cut into wood, stone, antler or bone. Runes were used to make lists, write messages and carve people's names to remember them. Many Vikings believed that runes had magic powers.

Runes carved on wood.

Rus (Rooss)

Vikings from Sweden who went to live in Russia. At first, they were raiders and traders who sold furs and slaves. But they soon built towns and set up strong kingdoms.

Rus carrying their ship to avoid rocks in a Russian river.

saga

Long, exciting story about famous people or great adventures. Most Viking poems, stories and songs were not written down. Instead, people remembered them and passed them on. Rich Vikings paid skalds (poets) to compose new songs and perform old favourites.

ships

Vikings were expert sailors and built splendid ships. Some were war ships, some were little ferry boats, some were for trading and exploring. Viking ships were made of wood, by workers using simple hand tools. They were powered by men rowing or by the wind blowing into their sails. They were steered by a wooden oar at the stern (back).

Fast, sleek longships sailed on raids.

Trading ships had wide, deep hulls to carry lots of goods.

Ferry boats and rowing boats stayed close to the shore.

Ferry boat

Rowing boat

Ss slaves

Many Viking families had slaves. Some were foreigners, captured in war or on raids. Others were born to slave parents, or were made slaves as a punishment for crimes. Slaves could not own land or carry weapons.

Slaves could be sold, or even killed, by their owners.

Ss sports, toys and games

Sports were fun and good training for fighters. In summer, Vikings went swimming and fishing, ran races, rode horses, climbed mountains and wrestled. In winter, they went skating and skiing. Indoor games included juggling and hnefatafl (say *nher-eh-tah-full*) – a game like chess. Viking children played with toy weapons, dolls, bats and balls.

Board and counters for playing hnefatafl.

Thor

God of thunder and lightning. He was huge, strong, and stupid. Legends told how he fought against giants. Farmers and sailors wore lucky charms shaped like Thor's mighty hammer.

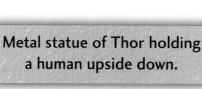

Metal statue of Thor holding a human upside down.

towns

Craftsmen and traders lived in towns. Rich customers came to buy goods from them. Viking kings built new towns with strong walls to keep traders safe. In return, townspeople paid the king taxes.

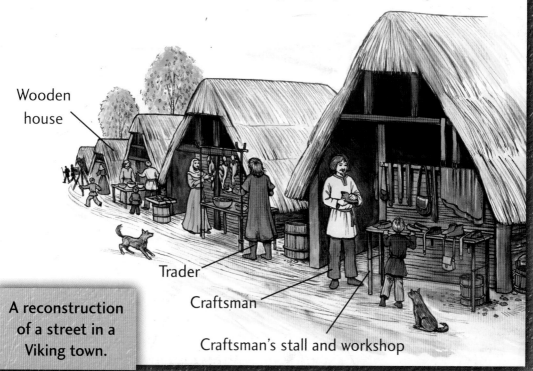

Wooden house

Trader

Craftsman

Craftsman's stall and workshop

A reconstruction of a street in a Viking town.

trade

Trade made Vikings rich. They sold goods from their own homelands, such as walrus teeth, seal skins, birds of prey, dried fish, amber, iron and timber. They also sold goods bought from far-away peoples, or captured on raids. These included beeswax, furs from Russia, wine, weapons, glass and pottery from France and Germany, and silk, spices and silver from the Middle East.

A Viking trader's scales

travel

Vikings travelled amazing distances to fight, trade, build new settlements or explore. They travelled by ship, walked, rode on horseback and used horses to pull carts with heavy loads. In winter, they travelled over snow on skis and sledges. There were few roads in Viking lands.

A wooden sledge decorated with carvings.

valkyries (Val-kear-eez)

Warrior goddesses who carried the spirits of brave dead warriors to live in Odin's palace, called Valhalla.

Silver model of a valkyrie. She is holding out a drink to welcome a dead warrior.

war

Vikings made shock attacks from ships, grabbing loot and killing anyone who tried to stop them. In battles on land, they lined up side by side, hurled spears and rushed towards their enemy. They believed that bravery was more important than staying alive.

Eager warriors rushing ashore.

weapons and armour

Swords were designed for slashing, spears for throwing, and battle-axes for hitting and hacking. The best were given names by their owners, such as 'killer snake' and 'wound-maker'. Warriors wore leather helmets and **tunics** and carried wooden shields. Kings and chiefs had metal helmets and tunics.

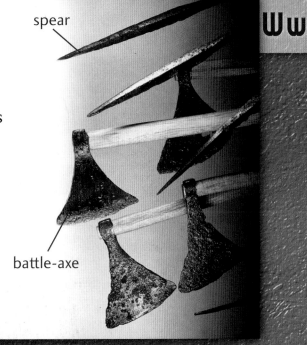

spear

battle-axe

weaving

Making cloth by twisting threads over and under each other. Viking women wove cloth using a big wooden frame, called a loom. They also spun thread, mostly from sheep's wool.

Woman weaving cloth on a loom

women

Viking women were strong and hard-working. They cared for their families and cooked and cleaned. They ran farms when men were away. Older women were respected and asked for their wise advice.

woodworking

There were many forests in the Vikings' lands and Vikings were skilled at making useful objects from wood. These included plates, drinking cups and children's toys, as well as bows and arrows, buckets and bridges.

The carved wooden prow (front end) of a Viking warship.

words

The Vikings took their language to lands where they settled. Today, we still use some Viking words in English, such as egg, sister, happy, knife, snarl and smile.

Yggdrasil (Ig-drah-sill)

According to Viking legends, Yggdrasil was a huge tree that supported the world. It was guarded by three goddesses. They decided how long each person would live.

Carved wooden doorway from Norway, showing Yggdrasil.

Glossary

Christian – a person who worships Jesus Christ

fungi – a group of plants which live off other plants or decaying matter, such as mushrooms and toadstools

Normans – Vikings who settled in a part of northern France. Today, the area is called Normandy

preserve – keep safe for future use. Vikings dried fruit in the sun, soaked fish in salty water, and, in winter, froze meat in the snow

raid – attack to steal and destroy

tunic – loose, baggy, usually knee-length piece of clothing, with sleeves

Yule – mid-winter festival which lasted for 12 days

Index